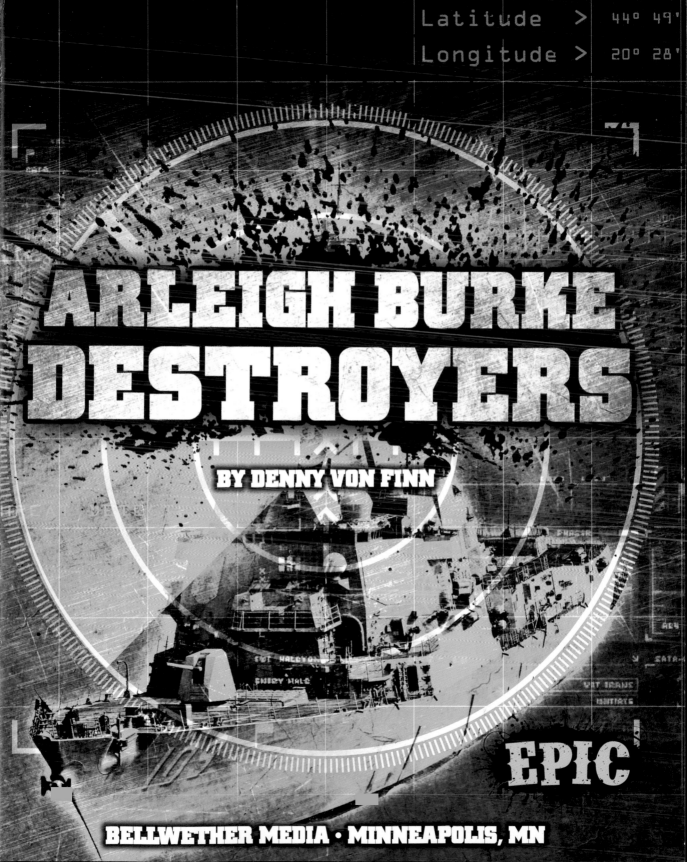

ARLEIGH BURKE DESTROYERS

BY DENNY VON FINN

EPIC

BELLWETHER MEDIA · MINNEAPOLIS, MN

EPIC

EPIC BOOKS are no ordinary books. They burst with intense action, high-speed heroics, and shadows of the unknown. Are you ready for an Epic adventure?

Range

0   50   100

This edition first published in 2014 by Bellwether Media, Inc.

No part of this publication may be reproduced in whole or in part without written permission of the publisher. For information regarding permission, write to Bellwether Media, Inc., Attention: Permissions Department, 5357 Penn Avenue South, Minneapolis, MN 55419.

Library of Congress Cataloging-in-Publication Data

Von Finn, Denny.
  Arleigh Burke Destroyers / by Denny Von Finn.
      pages cm. – (Epic: Military Vehicles)
  Includes bibliographical references and index.
  Summary: "Engaging images accompany information about Arleigh Burke Destroyers. The combination of high-interest subject matter and light text is intended for students in grades 2 through 7"– Provided by publisher.
  Audience: Grades 2-7.
  ISBN 978-1-62617-080-3 (hbk. : alk. paper)
  1. Destroyers (Warships)–United States–Juvenile literature. 2. Arleigh Burke (Destroyer)–Juvenile literature. 3. Guided missile ships–Juvenile literature. I. Title.
  V825.3.V66 2014
  623.825'4–dc23
                            2013034881

Printed in the United States of America, North Mankato, MN.

The photographs in this book are reproduced through the courtesy of the United States Department of Defense. A special thanks to Svitlana Kazachek for contributing the additional photo on p. 9 (small).

TABLE OF CONTENTS

ARLEIGH BURKE DESTROYERS

An Arleigh Burke **destroyer** is on the hunt. Its **sonar** finds an enemy **submarine**! Sailors race to their battle stations.

Destroyer Fact

An Arleigh Burke destroyer uses a cable that is 1 mile (1.6 kilometers) long to pull its sonar device!

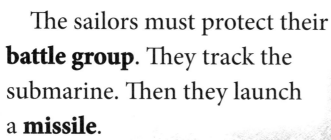

The sailors must protect their **battle group**. They track the submarine. Then they launch a **missile**.

MISSILE

The missile shoots into the sky. Seconds later, it splashes into the sea miles away. Direct hit! The destroyer's **mission** is complete.

THREAT DETECTED

70

CREW, WEAPONS, AND PARTS

Range

DECK

Arleigh Burkes are some of the largest destroyers ever built. Each has a crew of around 300 sailors. Many work below **deck** in the **Combat Information Center** (CIC).

COMBAT INFORMATION
CENTER (CIC)

The Arleigh Burke destroyer is armed with 90 missiles below deck. Their weight also keeps the ship stable in rough seas.

MISSILE

Destroyer Fact

Arleigh Burke destroyers also carry torpedoes and guns on board.

The Arleigh Burke destroyer also has a thick **hull**. It is made of steel. The hull cuts through big waves at high speeds.

Destroyer Fact

Arleigh Burke destroyers have room for two helicopters to land.

—— **HULL**

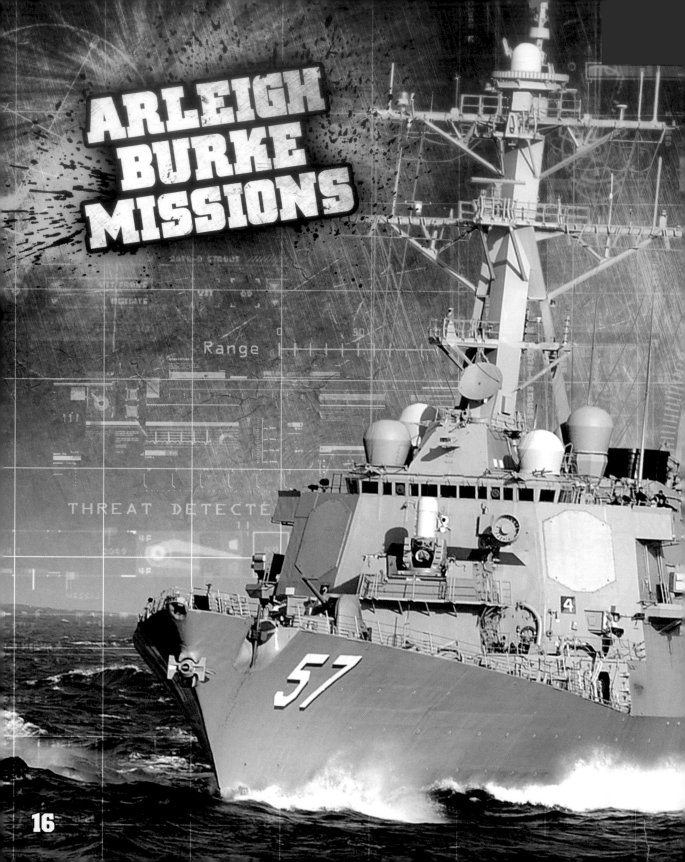

ARLEIGH BURKE MISSIONS

Arleigh Burke destroyers complete many missions. They protect other U.S. ships and attack enemy ships and planes.

Arleigh Burke destroyers also help the Army on land. They are used in the **War on Terror**. Their missiles destroy enemy tanks and trucks hundreds of miles away.

Range

Destroyer Fact

An Arleigh Burke destroyer has a gun that can aim and fire by itself.

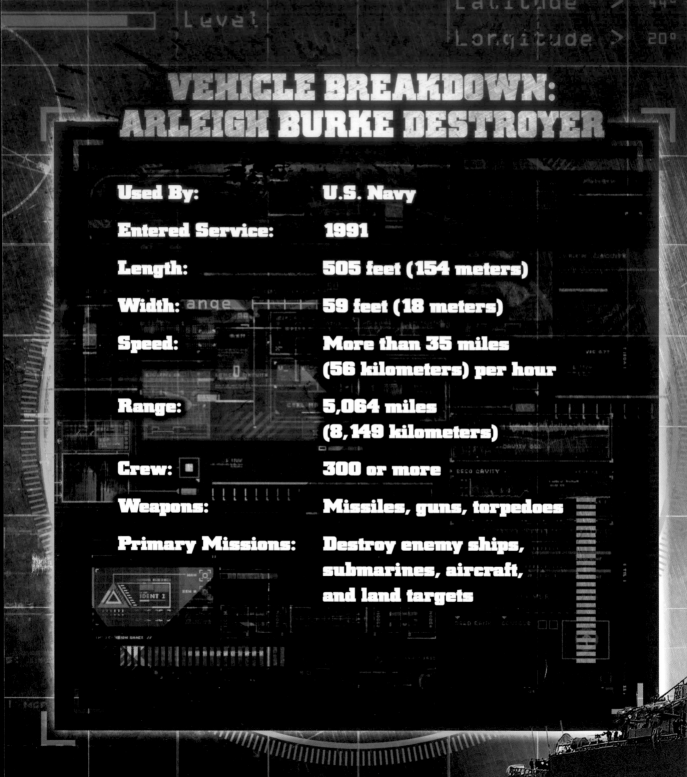

VEHICLE BREAKDOWN: ARLEIGH BURKE DESTROYER

Used By:	U.S. Navy
Entered Service:	1991
Length:	505 feet (154 meters)
Width:	59 feet (18 meters)
Speed:	More than 35 miles (56 kilometers) per hour
Range:	5,064 miles (8,149 kilometers)
Crew:	300 or more
Weapons:	Missiles, guns, torpedoes
Primary Missions:	Destroy enemy ships, submarines, aircraft, and land targets

Arleigh Burke destroyers can be found all over the world. Their brave crews protect people everywhere!

Destroyer Fact

The U.S. Navy has 62 Arleigh Burke destroyers.

GLOSSARY

battle group—war and supply ships that travel together

Combat Information Center (CIC)—the area below a destroyer's deck where the crew operates the radar and weapons

deck—the large, flat surface on top of a ship

destroyer—a fast Navy ship with many weapons; a destroyer is designed to attack enemy targets.

hull—the body of a ship that keeps it afloat

missile—an explosive that is guided to a target

mission—a military task

sonar—a system that uses sound waves to locate targets

submarine—a naval vessel that travels great distances underwater

War on Terror—a war led by the United States to stop organized groups from performing acts of violence; the War on Terror began in 2001.

TO LEARN MORE

At the Library

Alvarez, Carlos. *Arleigh Burke Destroyers*. Minneapolis, Minn.: Bellwether Media, 2010.

Hamilton, John. *Destroyers*. Minneapolis, Minn.: ABDO Pub., 2013.

Rustad, Martha E. H. *U.S. Navy Destroyers*. Mankato, Minn.: Capstone Press, 2007.

On the Web

Learning more about
Arleigh Burke destroyers
is as easy as 1, 2, 3.

1. Go to www.factsurfer.com.

2. Enter "Arleigh Burke destroyers" into the search box.

3. Click the "Surf" button and you will see a list
of related Web sites.

With factsurfer.com, finding more information
is just a click away.

INDEX